As of January 6, 2012, this guidance applies to federal savings associations in addition to national banks.*

I0448471

Comptroller of the Currency
Administrator of National Banks

Conflicts of Interest

Comptroller's Handbook

June 2000

AM

Asset Management

As of January 6, 2012, this guidance applies to federal savings associations in addition to national banks.*

Conflicts of Interest　　　　　Table of Contents

Conflicts of Interest   Introduction

A bank that provides asset management services for clients may be required to manage a variety of actual or potential conflicts of interest. Conflicts of interest and self-dealing transactions normally arise whenever the bank's ability to act exclusively in the best interest of account beneficiaries or clients is impaired. A fiduciary is required by a long history of case law to put the interests of account beneficiaries before the interests of the bank. The fiduciary owes its beneficiaries undivided loyalty and must administer each trust for the exclusive benefit of account beneficiaries and the purposes for which the account was created.

Conflicts of interest are not limited to instances in which the bank is acting as a fiduciary. In fact, as the trust business increasingly becomes an asset management business, the opportunities for a bank to find itself in a conflict of interest increase. Asset management — the management of third-party assets for a fee or commission — includes fiduciary services (personal, employee benefits, and corporate), investment advisory services, the retail sales of nondeposit investment products, and agency arrangements including custody of assets. When a national bank provides these services, the best interests of the client and the bank are not always the same.

This booklet provides guidance to examiners evaluating the risk management practices banks have in place to control conflicts of interest and self-dealing. The booklet's introduction provides an overview of risks and controls associated with conflicts of interest. The appendix contains a more in-depth discussion of certain transactions that may result in conflicts of interest or self-dealing. The procedures are designed to be used in large banks and, as needed, in community banks. In community banks, the procedures supplement the Comptroller's Handbook booklet "Community Bank Fiduciary Activities Supervision." For additional information, see this booklet's "References" page.

The Employee Retirement Income Security Act of 1974 (ERISA) views certain transactions as conflicts of interest and self-dealing. This booklet does not discuss those conflicts of interest in depth. Rather, it clarifies selected topics. The planned Comptroller's Handbook booklet "Retirement Plan Services" will contain a comprehensive discussion of conflicts of interest and self-dealing activities in accounts subject to ERISA. In the interim, examiners with questions concerning potential conflicts of interest in accounts subject to ERISA should consult with their district lead fiduciary experts or the Asset Management Division.

Types of Conflicts of Interest

Increasingly complex financial services, products, corporate organizations, affiliations, and arrangements with service providers may give rise to relationships that can result in conflicts of interest. Conflicts of interest and self-dealing activities may result from dealings involving insiders, the bank benefiting inappropriately, the bank's conflicting roles with a client, or an employee's unethical conduct.

National bank regulations identify certain activities involving a fiduciary that are generally not permissible. For example, 12 CFR 9.12, Self-Dealing and Conflicts of Interest, specifies certain investment, lending, and sales practices that are not generally permissible. 12 CFR 9.5(b), Policies and Procedures, requires banks to adopt and follow procedures adequate to ensure that fiduciary officers and employees do not misuse material nonpublic information. In addition, 12 CFR 12.7(a) requires banks to adopt certain securities trading policies and procedures.

In addition to these regulations, national banks may be subject to a variety of other laws, including applicable state law, rules and regulations of other federal regulators, and applicable interpretations issued by regulatory agencies. In particular, banks offering asset management activities may be subject to the rules and regulations of the Securities and Exchange Commission (SEC), Department of Labor (DOL), and the National Association of Securities Dealers, Inc. (NASD). The appendices to this booklet discuss some of these applicable laws, rules, and regulations in more detail.

Dealings Involving Insiders

Dealings with persons or entities connected with the bank in a way that might affect its judgment represent a potential conflict of interest or self-dealing activity. Such dealings may include investing in stock held by insiders (including bank officers, directors, and employees) or their related interests, assuming their obligations, acquiring their property, buying their trust property or accepting its transfer, or lending trust funds to them (12 USC 92a(h)). The

---

bank should develop policies and procedures to ensure that such dealings are monitored and restricted. Although some of these activities may be authorized by applicable state law or governing documents, policies and procedures often prohibit these potential conflicts or establish ways for the bank to avoid them. (See Appendix B, "Transactions between the Bank and Related Interests," for a more detailed discussion.)

Inappropriate Financial Benefit

Transactions with insiders may result in additional compensation, financial benefits, or goods and services for the bank as trustee. Particularly when these benefits are not properly authorized and disclosed, they represent improper conflicts of interest and self-dealing. Management must develop a process to identify all potentially inappropriate transactions; the process must ensure that conflicts are either avoided or properly authorized and disclosed.
A bank may gain an inappropriate financial benefit if it generates additional fee-based business for itself or an affiliate in one of the following ways: by using an affiliated company's income-producing services, by charging undisclosed fees to accounts for security transactions, or by receiving payment for other services that are normally included in fiduciary administration fees. If a bank fiduciary obtains financial benefits (including goods and services) from a service provider (whether affiliated or not), the benefits must be authorized and must not be provided in exchange for using that provider.

For more detailed discussions, see appendix A, "Use of Material Nonpublic Information"; appendix B, "Transactions between the Bank and Related Interests"; appendix C, "Trust Brokerage Allocation and Securities Trading"; appendix D, "Soft Dollars and Directed Commission Arrangements"; appendix G, "Reasonable Compensation"; and appendix H, "Fee Concessions."

Conflicting Roles and Responsibilities

Banks can serve in many different, and potentially conflicting, roles for their fiduciary clients. A bank's responsibilities as lender, credit enhancer, or security underwriter may run counter to its duties as fiduciary. Banks must identify and monitor conflicting responsibilities and communicate guidelines for preventing self-dealing and conflicts of interest. When a bank fiduciary has failed to prevent self-dealing or conflicts of interest and is not certain about what remedial action it should take, it should consult with legal counsel.

For more detailed discussions, see appendix E, "Use of Mutual Funds as Fiduciary Investments," and appendix F, "Unique Situations Posing Potential Conflicts."

Employees' Unethical Conduct

Employees' unethical conduct can undermine the fiduciary's ability to fulfill its duty of loyalty to account beneficiaries. A bank that promulgates a code of ethics for employees that clearly communicates the bank's expectations may reduce the risk of unethical conduct.

Bank management should have monitoring systems in place to detect employee conduct that conflicts with the bank's responsibilities as a fiduciary. Systems should be sufficient to alert the bank when a bank employee serves as co-fiduciary with the bank for a fee, competes with the bank, receives loans from fiduciary clients, accepts gifts or bequests from fiduciary clients, receives goods and services from vendors, or executes personal securities transactions that are counter to the best interests of account beneficiaries.

For a more detailed discussion, see appendix A, "Use of Material Nonpublic Information."

Authorization of Otherwise Impermissible Activities

In 12 CFR 9.12, several activities that would normally constitute conflicts of interest are deemed permissible if authorized by applicable law. Applicable law is defined in 12 CFR 9.2(b) as the law of a state or other jurisdiction governing a national bank's fiduciary relationships, any applicable federal law, the terms of the governing instrument, or any court order pertaining to the relationship.

State and local statutes and interpretations may authorize transactions that would otherwise be prohibited as conflicts of interest or self-dealing. A corporate trustee should not rely on a general authorization to conduct an otherwise impermissible transaction, unless the general authorization has been interpreted specifically to permit such a transaction in the courts of the state in which the trustee is located.

Specific provisions of the trust agreement may authorize or direct the bank fiduciary to transact types of business at its own discretion that would otherwise be impermissible. Broad general investment language commonly found in trust agreements is not sufficient to authorize an investment that results in a conflict of interest or self-dealing by the fiduciary. The trust agreement must specifically authorize the type of transaction or investment. However, a general power of authority to hold original investments has been widely held to permit retention of investments which otherwise create a conflict of interest.

A court order may protect a fiduciary from liability by authorizing a conflict of interest or self-dealing. When seeking a court order, a national bank must fully and accurately disclose to the court all pertinent facts about the conflict of interest or self-dealing. Only when the court has those facts can it render an informed decision. Such authorizations may not be effective in the absence of full disclosure and proper notice to all beneficiaries. A specific court order applies only to the detailed circumstances as presented to the court. It may not insulate a bank from liability for a breach of trust committed subsequent to the court action.

In certain circumstances, a trustee is permitted to enter into a transaction posing an otherwise impermissible conflict. Such a transaction must be fair and executed in the beneficiaries' best interest. Proper consent of all beneficiaries is required. To obtain proper consent, the bank must fully and completely disclose the facts about the conflict.

Obtaining the consent of all beneficiaries may be difficult, because more than one class of remaindermen may exist. If beneficiaries are minors, unborn, or otherwise unable to give informed consent, a guardian ad litem must be appointed for them to represent their interests in court, and an order approving the transaction must be obtained from the appropriate court.

In some circumstances, applicable law may be silent or appear ambiguous. In such cases, a bank may elect to obtain an opinion from its attorney. Although the opinion may help the bank understand an ambiguous law, the bank should avoid relying on an opinion of counsel as specific authorization for a questionable transaction. Before acting on such an opinion, the bank should evaluate fully the risks involved in the questionable transaction.

A grantor who reserves the power to modify or revoke a trust instrument is usually considered the absolute owner of the trust property. The grantor of a revocable trust can direct the fiduciary to conduct otherwise impermissible transactions, unless the activity is illegal. If the grantor requests a transaction that would normally violate the rule of undivided loyalty, the bank should require that the trust agreement be amended to authorize the transaction or require the grantor to authorize each transaction in writing. Trust agreements that include provisions that relieve a fiduciary of responsibility for breaches of fiduciary duty have generally been held by local courts to be void.

The bank may seek guidance from an attorney to resolve a conflict of interest or self-dealing. In other circumstances, legal counsel may recommend that a bank cure a contingent or potential liability by making a sale or transfer that amounts to a conflict of interest or self-dealing. In such a case, the board of directors may formally approve the action and provide that the bank fully reimburse each account in cash for any losses from the transaction.

Risks and Controls

The Comptroller's Handbook booklet "Large Bank Supervision" established a framework for supervising banks by risk. Under the framework, examiners assess a bank's risk management system, including its effectiveness in identifying, measuring, controlling, and monitoring risk.

Risk is the potential that events, expected or unexpected, may have an adverse impact on the bank's earnings or capital. The OCC has defined nine categories of risk for bank supervision purposes. These risks, which are defined in the "Bank Supervision Process" and "Large Bank Supervision" booklets, are credit, interest rate, liquidity, price, foreign exchange, transaction, compliance, strategic, and reputation. These risks are not mutually exclusive; any product or service may expose the bank to multiple risks. For analysis and discussion, however, the OCC identifies and assesses the risks separately.

A bank that does not properly manage conflicts of interest and self-dealing may be exposed to heightened compliance, reputation, and strategic risk.

Compliance Risk

Compliance risk is the risk to earnings or capital arising from violations or nonconformance with laws, rules, regulations, prescribed practices, or ethical standards. The risk also arises in situations where the laws or rules governing certain bank products or activities of the bank's clients may be ambiguous or untested. Compliance risk exposes the institution to fines, civil money penalties, payment of damages, and the voiding of contracts. Compliance risk can lead to a diminished reputation, reduced franchise value, limited business opportunities, lessened expansion potential, and lack of contract enforceability.

The rules, regulations, and laws governing fiduciary activities are voluminous and complex. To minimize the risk of noncompliance, banks must create strong risk management systems to avoid even the appearance of conflicts of interest. Conflicts of interest or self-dealing may result in costly, highly publicized litigation. Regardless of its outcome, a long legal battle can jeopardize a bank's present and future earnings. Fines, judgments, and settlements to avoid litigation can further deplete earnings.

Reputation Risk

Reputation risk is the risk to earnings or capital arising from negative public opinion. This affects the institution's ability to establish new relationships or services, or continue servicing existing relationships. This risk can expose the institution to litigation, financial loss, or damage to its reputation. Reputation risk exposure is present throughout the organization and is why banks have the responsibility to exercise an abundance of caution in dealing with their customers and community. This risk is present in such activities as asset management and agency transactions.

Actual or implied conflicts of interest and self-dealing transactions can affect a bank's reputation negatively by jeopardizing a client's trust. Loss of client trust because of a bank's questionable loyalty may threaten to erode its customer base. Deposit accounts, loan relationships, corporate clients, and other banking relationships may be lost as a result.

Strategic Risk

Strategic risk is the risk to earnings or capital arising from adverse business decisions or improper implementation of those decisions. This risk is a function of the compatibility between an organization's strategic goals, the business strategies developed to achieve those goals, the resources deployed against these goals, and the quality of implementation. The resources needed to carry out business strategies are both tangible and intangible. They include communication channels, operating systems, delivery networks, and managerial capacities and capabilities.

Banks are relying increasingly on fee-based activities as a stable, consistent source of revenue. If a bank is unable to realize its fiduciary goals, its overall strategic plan and direction may be affected negatively. A bank's ability to realize its strategic goals may depend upon its success in cultivating and maintaining a satisfied, loyal customer base. A bank, because of unauthorized conflicts of interest and self-dealing, may threaten the stability of its fiduciary client base and be unable to fund businesses or attain growth projections and goals.

Internal Controls

Asset management clients, both institutional and individual, expect an asset manager to be honest and ethical. To meet industry standards, many banks implement stringent controls. When evaluating internal controls, examiners consider the control environment; risk assessment systems; control activities; accounting, information, and communication processes; and self-assessment and monitoring systems.

To manage the risks associated with conflicts of interest and self-dealing, the bank must have systems in place that first identify actual or potential conflicts. Policies reflecting the bank's willingness to accept the associated risks should be established and followed. Because of the importance of a sound reputation in the asset management business, many banks take steps to prevent actual conflicts of interest and also to minimize the appearance of conflicts of interests. Some common controls include:

- Assessment of business lines and activities to identify all potential conflicts of interest and self-dealing.

- Identification of all insiders and their related interests.

- Development of written policies and procedures appropriate to the size and complexity of the bank's business. Policies and procedures should establish an ethics policy, identify prohibited activities, and offer guidelines for avoiding or managing conflicts of interest and self-dealing.

- Dissemination of information on conflicts of interest and self-dealing to enable supervisory committees and officers to:
  - Identify existing or potential problems when an account is considered for acceptance as well as when one already on the books is reviewed.
  - Recognize the legality of certain conflicts or potential conflicts.
  - Monitor potential conflicts of interest and self-dealing.
  - Evaluate the level of risk to the bank.

- A risk control process, including audit, compliance, and training programs, that emphasizes the importance of avoiding conflicts of interest and self-dealing.

Refer to the Comptroller's Handbook booklet "Internal Controls" for a more thorough discussion.

Conflicts of Interest   Examination Procedures

General Procedures

These procedures are intended to determine whether the bank's policies, procedures, and internal controls are adequate with respect to conflicts of interest and self-dealing. The examiner's assessment of risk should determine how much testing and how many procedures should be performed. This assessment should consider work performed by other regulatory agencies, internal/external auditors, and internal compliance review systems. The assessment should evaluate formalized policies and procedures, internal controls, and management information systems.

Objective: To set the scope for assessing the quantity of risk and the quality of risk management over conflicts of interest.

1. Review the following documents to identify any previously identified problems.

   - Supervisory strategy in the OCC's electronic information system.
   - Previous examination report.
   - Overall summary comments.
   - Work papers from the previous examination.
   - Audit reports and, if appropriate, working papers.
   - Compliance reports.

2. Determine, during early discussions with management:

   - How the bank identifies and monitors potential conflicts and how actual conflicts are customarily resolved.
   - Any significant changes in policies, practices, personnel, or control systems.
   - Any internal or external factors that could affect conflicts of interest.

3. Obtain and review reports management uses to supervise conflicts of interest. Discern any material changes since the previous examination. Some of the reports typically available to management are:

    - A list of all insiders and related interests as defined in 12 CFR 9.12(a)(1).
    - A list of all significant (potential or actual) fiduciary conflicts of interest and self-dealing of which bank management is aware.
    - A list of all accounts owning proprietary (bank-advised) mutual funds and mutual funds that pay the bank a fee, bank time deposits, bank certificates of deposits, bank or holding company stock or debt instruments, and securities of related interests.
    - A list of approved brokers and the policy and basis for selecting those brokers.
    - A copy of the approved securities list for managed accounts including management comments supporting the purchase of securities that are not on the approved list.
    - A copy of the most recent audit and compliance reports, with management responses to any concerns raised in those reports.
    - A copy of the audit and compliance program.
    - A list of all financial benefits the bank receives from third parties, such as servicers and investment companies. This information may be included on the bank's income and fee reports.

4. Determine the potential for conflicts of interest and self-dealing by considering:

    - The nature of products and services offered.
    - The complexity of the corporate structure and dealings with affiliates and subsidiaries.
    - The use of affiliated pooled or proprietary mutual funds, mutual funds for which the bank receives fees, cash management products, data processing services, depository services, investment management services, and other services.
    - Policies and procedures for conflicts and self-dealing.
    - Internal assessments of risk and the risk management program conducted by management, compliance, or audit functions of the bank.

- The bank's history of avoiding conflicts and resolving them in favor of beneficiaries.

5.   Using the information you gained by performing the previous steps, make a preliminary risk assessment and consult with the EIC and other appropriate supervisors to establish the examination's scope and objectives.

Select from among the following examination procedures the steps that are necessary to meet those objectives. An examination will seldom require every step to be performed. The examiner should coordinate this review with the examiners evaluating account and asset administration to avoid duplication of efforts.

6.   As examination procedures are performed, test for compliance with established policies or procedures and the existence of appropriate internal control processes. Identify any area with inadequate supervision or undue risk, and discuss with the EIC the need to perform additional procedures. For those examination procedures not performed, document why. (For example, the subject area was not within the scope of the examination, or specified examination areas were not applicable to the bank's range of activities.)

Quantity of Risk

Conclusion: The quantity of risk is (low, moderate, high).

To develop an overall conclusion on the quantity of risk, the examiner should first evaluate the quantity of compliance, reputation, and strategic risks. Only after quantifying those three risks should the examiner come to an overall conclusion on the quantity of risk.

Compliance Risk

Compliance risk is often encountered in asset management activities, largely because of the potential for conflicts of interest inherent in the many asset management services banks provide. A bank controls compliance risk by following sound fiduciary principles, prudent ethical standards, internal policies and procedures, and the terms of client documents and other contracts.

Objective: Determine the quantity and direction of compliance risk from asset management activities that give rise to actual or potential conflicts of interest. Determine:

1. The nature and extent of business activities, including new products and services, that may have an impact upon compliance risk.

2. The amount and significance of litigation and customer complaints.

3. The volume and significance of noncompliance and nonconformance with policies and procedures, laws, regulations, prescribed practices, and ethical standards.

4. Whether you must sample accounts to verify compliance with relevant laws and regulations. Consider identified weaknesses in internal controls, audit, compliance, or risk management systems when making your decision. Some of the relevant laws and regulations are:

   • 12 USC 61• prohibits a bank as sole trustee from voting bank stock in the election of directors;

- 12 USC 92a(h) • prohibits lending fiduciary assets to bank officers, directors, and employees;

- 12 CFR 9.5 • requires a bank exercising fiduciary powers to adopt and follow internal controls regarding brokerage placement practices, prevents misuse of material inside information, and prevents self-dealing and conflicts of interest;

- 12 CFR 9.10 • prohibits bank fiduciary with investment discretion or discretion over distributions from allowing funds awaiting investment or distribution to remain uninvested and undistributed any longer than is reasonable for the proper management of the account and consistent with applicable law;

- 12 CFR. 9.12 • prohibits self-dealing and conflicts of interest; and

- 12 CFR 9.15 • limits bank fiduciary compensation unless set or governed by applicable law.

Reputation Risk

Because a sound reputation is essential for success as an asset manager, many banks are extremely careful to minimize both real and potential conflicts of interest. The examiner's estimation of the quantity of reputation risk depends on the level of compliance risk and the quality of the bank's risk management systems.

Objective: Determine the quantity and direction of reputation risk arising from asset management activities that give rise to actual or potential conflicts of interest. (For guidance, refer to the "Asset Management" and "Large Bank Supervision" booklets of the Comptroller's Handbook.)

1. Evaluate the impact of strategic and external factors on the quantity of reputation risk. Consider how management, processes, and systems affect reputation risk. (The evaluation factors are listed in the "Asset Management" and "Large Bank Supervision" booklets of the Comptroller's Handbook.)

Strategic Risk

To evaluate strategic risk, an examiner should consider the levels of reputation and compliance risk in relation to the bank's strategic objectives. For example, a moderate amount of reputation and compliance risk may be insignificant to a bank that derives only a small percentage of its revenues from asset management activities and has no plans to change its product mix or major business lines.

Conversely, a moderate amount of reputation and compliance risk may significantly increase strategic risk if the bank derives a significant amount of income from asset management activities or plans to grow or expand its asset management business lines. It is essential that an examiner view all of a bank's risks, not just its strategic risk, from the perspective of the bank's strategic goals.

Objective: Determine the quantity and direction of strategic risk arising from asset management activities that give rise to actual or potential conflicts of interest. (Refer to the "Asset Management" and "Large Bank Supervision" booklets of the Comptroller's Handbook for guidance.)

1. Discuss with management the strategic objectives the bank has established for asset management activities.

2. Evaluate the results obtained from conducting the previous procedures to determine whether any weaknesses were identified that may hamper the bank's ability to achieve its strategic goals.

3. Consider the quantity of reputation and compliance risk resulting from asset management activities and determine the overall quantity of strategic risk.

Quality of Risk Management

Conclusion: The quality of risk management
is (strong, satisfactory, weak).

Policy

Objective: Determine the adequacy of policies and procedures developed to control the risks associated with conflicts of interest and self-dealing.

1. Review policies to determine that those required by applicable laws and regulations have been written. Consider the requirements of:

    *   12 CFR 9.5,
    *   12 CFR 12.7(a),
    *   ERISA, and
    *   Industry standards relating to insider activities and employee ethics.

2. Review policies and procedures to determine whether they are consistent with the size and complexity of the institution's asset management activities.

3. Review your findings from the "Quantity of Risk" section of these procedures to determine whether policies and procedures are adequate. Consider the number and significance of any exceptions to policy and procedure, as well as circumstances not addressed by formal policies and procedures.

Processes

Objective: Determine the effectiveness of internal controls designed to ensure compliance with 12 USC 92a(h).

1. Determine that controls are in place to prevent the lending of fiduciary assets to bank officers, directors, and employees.

Objective: Determine the effectiveness of internal controls designed to ensure compliance with 12 CFR 9.5.

1. Review the bank's written policy regarding brokerage placement practices (12 CFR 9.5(a)). Determine that:

   - Brokerage fees and allocations are monitored.
   - Brokerage fees are not subject to depository, soft-dollar commitments, kickbacks, or other compensation arrangements that would impair the best judgment of the bank or prevent the best execution of trades.
   - Trades are fair and equitably allocated to all accounts.

2. Review the bank's written policy designed to ensure that fiduciary officers and employees do not misuse material inside information (12 CFR 9.5(b)).

3. Review the bank's written policy designed to prevent self-dealing and conflicts of interest (12 CFR 9.5(c)) and the ethics standards established for employees. Determine that personnel properly acknowledge those standards and that the standards address:

   - Personal trading, based on information gained as an employee of the bank, that conflicts with the best interests of beneficiaries, e.g., front-running.
   - Receiving goods and services from vendors (Banking Circular 233, "Acceptance of Financial Benefits by Bank Trust Departments").
   - Serving as co-fiduciary with the bank for a fee (12 CFR 9.15(b)).
   - Receiving loans from fiduciary clients.
   - Accepting gifts and bequests from fiduciary clients.

Objective: Determine the effectiveness of internal controls designed to ensure compliance with 12 CFR 12.7(a).

1. Determine that policies and procedures have been developed for bank officers and employees who are involved in the investment selection or recommendation process. Policies and procedures must:

- Assign responsibility for supervision of officers and employees who:
  - Transmit or place orders with registered broker/dealers.
  - Direct transactions in securities for customers.
  - Process orders or perform other related back-office functions.
- Provide for the fair and equitable allocation of securities and prices to accounts.
- Provide for the crossing of buy and sell orders on a fair and equitable basis.
- Require certain bank officers and employees involved in investment selection to report personal securities transactions made by them or on their behalf.

Objective: Determine the effectiveness of internal controls designed to ensure compliance with 12 CFR 9.12.

1. Evaluate internal controls designed to restrict sales and lending of fiduciary assets to related parties and ensure that any such sale or loan:

   - Is authorized by applicable law;
   - Exposes the bank to no more than contingent liability, according to legal counsel;
   - Is in accordance with the provisions of 12 CFR 9.12(a)(1); and
   - Complies with OCC requirements.

2. Determine that internal controls restrict the following transactions to those that are authorized by applicable law:

   - Selling assets (cross-trading) that the bank holds as fiduciary in one account to itself as fiduciary in another account (12 CFR 9.12(d) and 12 CFR 12.7(a)(3)).
   - Lending fiduciary assets to an account from funds belonging to another account (12 CFR 9.12(e)).
   - Lending to fiduciary accounts by the bank or its affiliates (12 CFR 9.12(c)).

- Loans by accounts over which the bank exercises investment responsibility, determining whether the borrower used the proceeds to repay a loan to the bank.
- The pledging of account assets to secure loans held by the bank or its affiliates, determining whether:
  - Conflicts are disclosed properly.
  - Pledged assets contain common or collective investment fund units, bank stock, or proprietary mutual funds.
  - The account is subject to ERISA.

3. Determine that internal controls are adequate to ensure that the following items have been purchased, retained, or sold in accordance with 12 CFR 9.12(a) or other applicable law:

   - Stock in the bank, holding company, or an affiliate; debentures and obligations; interest-bearing time or demand deposits; or repurchase agreements.
   - Stock and obligations of other organizations whose relationship with the bank may interfere with the bank's exercise of its best judgment. Such organizations may include companies in which directors or officers of the bank, its affiliates, or related organizations hold an interest.
   - Obligations of directors, officers, and employees of the bank, as well as obligations of directors and principal officers of its affiliates and related organizations.

Objective: Determine the effectiveness of the process used to ensure that uninvested trust funds are managed properly in accordance with 12 CFR 9.10.

1. Consider whether:
   - Funds awaiting investment or distribution remain uninvested or undistributed any longer than is reasonable or in compliance with applicable law.

- A bank that has investment discretion obtains a rate of return for funds awaiting investment or distribution that is consistent with applicable law.

Objective: Determine that controls over fees charged are in compliance with 12 CFR 9.15 or other applicable law.

1. Consider whether:
   - Fees are reasonable or in compliance with applicable law and properly disclosed.
   - Management obtains proper authorization for charging cash sweep or termination fees.
   - Bank employees acting as co-fiduciaries receive a fee. (When this relationship and compensation exist, they should be addressed by bank policy and must be specifically approved by the bank's board of directors.)
   - Revisions or changes in fees charged to accounts with set or fixed fee schedules were appropriate and properly authorized.
   - Any fee concessions for officers, directors, and other employees are granted under a general policy that is uniformly applied and approved by the board.
   - Management income and fee reports disclose unusual or improper fees.

Objective: Determine the effectiveness of the process the bank uses to ensure compliance with 12 USC 61 in voting its own bank stock, and determine whether the bank abides by applicable law when voting shares of its own bank holding company stock when electing directors. In addition, for companies in which directors, officers, employees, or related organizations have an interest that might interfere with the bank's exercise of its best judgment, determine whether the bank considers the best interests of beneficiaries when deciding how to vote proxies.

1. When trust accounts hold own bank stock, consider whether bank processes prevent voting by bank of its own stock and, when applicable, bank holding company stock and the stock of related interests or bank insiders.

Objective: Determine the effectiveness of internal controls designed to ensure compliance with other applicable law, including the governing instruments, state and local law, federal securities laws and regulations, and other federal requirements including ERISA and the Trust Indenture Act.

1. Determine whether the bank has controls to ensure that soft dollar payments or arrangements are consistent with the safe harbor provisions established by section 28(e) of the Securities Exchange Act of 1934 and that management makes a good faith determination that any brokerage fees received are reasonable relative to the services provided.

2. Determine that the bank, when acting as corporate bond trustee, performs an adequate check for conflicts of interest as required by the Trust Indenture Act of 1939 and part 9.

3. Determine whether the bank receives fees for providing administrative, shareholder, or subtransfer agent services to investment companies (mutual funds) in addition to 92a(h) normal account fees. Determine whether such fees are appropriate. Consider whether the fees are disclosed to beneficiaries, properly authorized, or equitably returned to accounts if required.

4. Evaluate the system used by the bank to ensure that:
    *   When the bank invests discretionary fiduciary assets in a mutual fund that either is proprietary (bank-advised) or pays the bank a fee, applicable law authorizes the transaction and the fund's objectives suit the account's needs;
    *   Disclosure and acknowledgment requirements applicable to both discretionary and non-discretionary accounts subject to ERISA are consistent with DOL Prohibited Transaction Class Exemption 77-4 and subsequent guidance; and
    *   The evaluation of proprietary mutual fund holdings is consistent with the evaluation of other asset holdings and complies with 12 CFR part 9.

---

5.   If the bank uses an affiliated broker to effect securities transactions for fiduciary accounts, determine that:

- Applicable law does not prohibit the use of an affiliated broker to effect securities transactions.
- The bank's payment of affiliated broker's fees for effecting brokerage transactions cover the cost of effecting the transaction and no more. Under no circumstances, unless authorized by applicable law, should the bank or its brokerage affiliate profit from a securities transaction effected for a fiduciary account.
- The bank's records establish, through a detailed cost analysis, that the amount of the fee charged by the affiliated broker is justified by the cost of the securities transactions executed. All fees paid to an affiliated broker should be clearly disclosed. The bank should also ensure, when applicable, that the affiliated broker adheres to the NASD's best execution requirement (NASD Rule 2320).

6.   If the bank sponsors limited real estate partnership syndications for its accounts, evaluate:

- Policies and practices related to account participation in the syndications.
- Disclosure and authorization of fees.
- The role of the bank, or a related interest, in the syndicate. Is the bank a general partner or a participant?

7.   Review information on debt securities that are issued by companies in which bank directors and principal officers hold an interest when such securities are also held in accounts for which the bank has investment discretion. Determine whether the issuer used the proceeds of any purchased security, held as a trust asset, to pay off any loan by the commercial department or to retire any securities of the issuer held by the commercial department. Examiners should check the prospectus or memoranda of a security issue for information on the use of the proceeds.

8. Determine that the bank has a process to ensure that it does not benefit financially from depository rebates or expense credits that it receives from depositories used for fiduciary funds.

9. Ascertain whether the bank or an affiliate has been a member of a syndicate that sold debt securities or whether the bank or an affiliate advised a party in a private placement or assisted in that placement. Using a list of such syndicates and private placements since the previous examination, determine whether:

   • Fiduciary investment personnel were notified of the bank's participation in such securities activities (12 USC 371c-1).
   • Any such securities were purchased by a fiduciary account.
     - Was the bank, or a bank affiliate, a principal underwriter in the underwriting syndicate?
     - If so, was there appropriate board approval or authorization of the purchase?
     - Were bond proceeds used to retire loans at the bank in full or in part?

10. Review instances when the bank serves in multiple capacities as trustee, letter of credit issuer, credit enhancer, or remarketing agent on corporate bonds and determine that such accounts are properly monitored, receive close supervision, and are documented adequately to ensure that the bank fulfills its fiduciary responsibilities.

Personnel

Objective: Determine whether bank management/personnel possess and display acceptable knowledge and technical skills in managing and performing duties related to conflicts of interest.

1. Assess the knowledge and technical skills of bank personnel, including management, related to conflicts of interest. Base your conclusions on what you learned while performing the foregoing procedures.

2. Review any educational programs conducted by the bank to foster awareness of the importance of avoiding both the appearance of a conflict and actual conflicts and self-dealing.

3. Discuss with management the system it uses to ensure that employees meet the ethical standards established by the bank.

Controls

Objective: Determine that management has instituted control systems appropriate to the type and levels of risk arising from conflicts of interest.

1. Consult with the examiner reviewing internal/external audit to evaluate audit coverage of issues related to conflicts of interest and self-dealing.

2. Consult with the examiner reviewing bank compliance management or risk management systems to determine that they are effective.

3. Evaluate any additional control systems implemented by the bank.

4. Determine that management is responsive to weaknesses or deficiencies identified by the control systems.

5. Determine that management information systems are capable of accurately gathering and tracking control system exceptions and providing needed reports.

Conclusions

Objective: To communicate findings and initiate corrective action on conflicts of interest or self-dealing when policies, practices, procedures, objectives, or internal controls are deficient or when violations of law, rulings, or regulations have been noted.

1. Provide the EIC with a brief conclusion regarding:

    *   The adequacy of risk management systems, including policies, processes, personnel, and control systems.
    *   Bank conformance to established policies and procedures.
    *   Internal control deficiencies or exceptions.
    *   Significant violations of laws, rules, or regulations.
    *   Corrective action recommended for identified deficiencies.
    *   The adequacy of MIS.
    *   Quantity of risk and quality of risk management associated with conflicts of interest and self-dealing.
    *   The overall level of compliance with applicable law, accepted industry standards, and bank policies and procedures, to assist the EIC in determining the compliance rating.
    *   Other matters of significance.

2. Identify significant risks. Assess the impact of management's control of conflicts of interest on the bank's aggregate risk and the direction of its risk. Specifically comment on the following risks: reputation, strategic, and compliance. Examiners should refer to guidance provided under the OCC's large bank risk assessment programs.

    *   Risk Categories: Compliance, Reputation, Strategic
    *   Risk Conclusions: High, Moderate, or Low
    *   Risk Direction: Increasing, Stable, or Decreasing

3. Determine, in consultation with the EIC, whether the risks identified are of enough significance to bring them to the board's

attention in the report of examination. If so, prepare items for inclusion in "Matters Requiring Board Attention" (MRBA).

- The MRBA should cover practices that:
  - Deviate from sound principles and may result in potential financial liability if not resolved.
  - Result in substantive noncompliance with laws.
- The MRBA should discuss:
  - Causes of the problem.
  - Consequences of inaction.
  - Management's commitment to corrective action.
  - The time frame and person(s) responsible for corrective action.

4. Discuss findings with bank management, addressing:

- Adequacy of risk management systems, including policies, processes, personnel, and control systems.
- Violations of law, rulings, regulations, or significant internal control deficiencies, emphasizing their causes and the potential for risks associated with fiduciary activities.
- Recommended corrective action for deficiencies cited.
- Bank's commitment to specific actions for correcting deficiencies.

5. As appropriate, prepare a brief comment on conflicts of interest for the report of examination. In general terms, address the following subjects:

- Quantity of risk.
- Quality of risk management.

6. Prepare a memorandum or update the work program with any information that will facilitate future examinations.

7. Update the OCC's electronic information system.

8. Organize and reference working papers in accordance with OCC guidance. Working papers should clearly and adequately support the conclusions reached.

Conflicts of Interest   Appendix A

Use of Material Nonpublic Information

Regulation 12 CFR 9.5(b) requires national banks exercising fiduciary powers to adopt and follow written policies and procedures adequate to ensure that fiduciary officers and employees do not use material nonpublic information in connection with any decision or recommendation to purchase or sell any security.

A so-called Chinese wall should prevent the passage of material inside information between a bank's fiduciary department and its commercial department in violation of securities laws and regulations, as well as fiduciary standards (see, e.g., Scott and Fratcher, The Law of Trusts, section 170.23A). But this wall should not be considered an absolute barrier. The doctrine does not require the total separation of fiduciary and commercial functions within a bank, nor does it prohibit the joint marketing and servicing of customers. Rather, it is intended to prevent the use of significant nonpublic information in making investment decisions.

The fiduciary may obtain material nonpublic information from a variety of sources, including employees' personal relationships, commercial lending relationships, transfer agent activities, and industry contacts. Management must take reasonable measures to prevent the inappropriate use of material nonpublic information to make fiduciary investment decisions, regardless of how the information was obtained.

The Insider Trading and Securities Fraud Enforcement Act of 1988 increased the maximum penalty for insider trading and use of material inside information to the greater of $1 million, or three times the profit gained or loss avoided as a result of the unlawful purchase, sale, or communication, and 10 years imprisonment. If a bank employee engages in insider trading, penalties may be assessed against the employee, the employee's manager, and the bank. In addition, banks and management-level employees may be found liable if they fail to take appropriate action to prevent insider trading. Although the act does not specify what actions are appropriate, banks are expected to adopt policies and procedures restricting the use of nonpublic information. The improper use of insider information may also expose bank employees, and the bank itself, to OCC administrative actions and possible civil litigation.

Conflicts of Interest   Appendix B

Transactions between Bank and Related Interests (Parties)

Prohibitions on Investments

Unless authorized by applicable law, a trustee bank that has discretion over the investment of a fiduciary account's funds is prohibited (12 CFR 9.12(a)) from investing in the stock and obligations of, or assets acquired from:

- The bank or any of its directors, officers, or employees.

- Affiliates of the bank or any of their directors, officers, or employees.

- Other individuals or entities with whom there exists an interest that might affect the bank's exercise of its best judgment.

In addition, a fiduciary account's investments in the following assets may give rise to a conflict of interest, unless authorized by applicable law:

- Investment companies (mutual funds) sponsored or advised by the bank or its affiliates.

- Time or savings deposits of the trustee bank, holding company, affiliates, or other organizations that are so connected as to possibly affect the bank's exercise of its best judgment.

- Loans originated by the bank.

Investing in or retaining shares of the trustee bank's stock places the trustee in a position of conflict. A trustee's decision whether to buy, sell, or retain shares of its own stock may not have the same objectivity as a decision whether to buy, sell, or retain other securities. A trustee cannot purchase shares of its own stock or related interest holdings unless properly authorized by applicable law. This is true even if the purchase is otherwise a proper fiduciary investment. Broad investment powers granted to the trustee in the trust agreement do not authorize the bank to purchase its own stock or other obligations.

When state statutes specifically authorize a corporate trustee to retain shares of its own stock received from the grantor, the trustee may rely on these statutes as authority for retaining those shares, if the shares would otherwise be a proper fiduciary investment. Some state statutes that generally authorize retention of securities owned by the testator at his death may be unclear about whether the trustee is authorized to retain its own stock. Accordingly, general retention statutes should not be viewed as sufficient protection for the corporate trustee, unless the courts of the state in which the trustee is located have held that their statute authorizes retention of the bank's own stock.

Frequently, bank trustees reduce holdings of their own bank stock or that of their holding company when the holdings represent a concentration of outstanding shares. A concentration is generally considered to be 10 per cent or more of all outstanding shares.

When the trust agreement does not refer to the shares of the trustee bank, but contains general authorization to retain original investments, the trustee may generally retain shares received in kind at the creation of the trust. A general authorization in the trust agreement to retain original investments has been widely held to be a waiver of the rule of undivided loyalty, provided the shares are otherwise a proper trust investment.

The existence of co-trustees may affect the bank's decision to sell or retain its own stock. The bank, as trustee, should obtain a directive from its co-trustee to retain the bank's stock if the co-trustee is the sole beneficiary. If other beneficiaries exist, the bank must not rely upon a co-trustee's directions and must refer to applicable law.

National banks that hold their own bank stock as a trustee are bound by their fiduciary obligations when voting that stock. Under 12 USC 61, national banks are prohibited from voting shares of stock they hold as trustee in the election of bank directors. However, if the trust agreement specifically reserves to an account's grantor or beneficiaries the power to determine how the shares of the trustee bank's stock will be voted, the shares of stock may be voted. The restrictions of 12 USC 61 do not apply to holding company stock.

Loans to Officers, Directors, and Employees

Twelve USC 92a(h) expressly prohibits a national bank from lending any funds from the fiduciary accounts it administers to the bank's officers, directors, or employees. If any bank officer, director, or employee makes or receives any such loan, that person may be fined up to $5,000, imprisoned, or both. In addition, the OCC may bring enforcement actions against the bank and its officers, directors, and employees, including the imposition of civil money penalties. (See OCC Bulletin 98-32, "Civil Money Penalties.")

When a bank officer makes such a loan or receives such a loan's proceeds, both the officer and the bank have committed a crime. For the bank to violate this statute, it need only be the trustee of funds that are lent to the officer, director, or employee. The fact that the transaction was executed at the direction of one or more persons does not make the bank any less culpable.

No exceptions to this prohibition are allowed under 12 USC 92a(h). The statute prevails over any instrument authority, beneficiary consent, or court order purporting to authorize the transaction. However, this strict statutory prohibition (carrying criminal sanctions) against lending trust assets to bank employees and insiders does not extend to their related interests or to bank affiliates.

Obligations of directors, officers, or employees received in kind are not prohibited by 12 USC 92a(h) unless they are renewed or carried past due at the bank's discretion. Demand loans of directors, officers, or employees received in kind should be paid within a reasonable time. A bank acting as executor of a will should not transfer such obligations to itself as trustee under the will. In an estate, repayment should normally occur within the usual period of administration.

Loans to Other Related Parties

When authorized by applicable law, a national bank fiduciary may lend funds to related parties who are not officers, directors, or employees. However, the bank's sole consideration should be the needs of the accounts involved and the best interests of the holders of beneficial interests. Even if specific authority permits a loan, the investment would be subject to criticism if it is not in the best interests of the account beneficiaries.

Loans to and from Fiduciary Accounts

While administering fiduciary accounts, a trustee may have to borrow funds to meet the needs of the account beneficiaries. National banks may generally make loans to a fiduciary account and hold a security interest in account assets if the transaction is fair to the account and is not prohibited by applicable law (see 12 CFR 9.12(c)). When a trust borrows from the trustee bank, the loan must be for the exclusive benefit of the trust beneficiaries and the loan's fees and interest rates must be reasonable.

An exception to the above standard applies to national banks administering a collective investment fund. Under 12 CFR 9.18(b)(8)(ii), the bank is prohibited from making a loan on the security of a participant's interest in the fund. An unsecured advance, however, until the next valuation date, may be permissible.

National banks are permitted to lend funds from one fiduciary account to another when the making of a loan is authorized by the trust agreement, fair to both accounts, and not prohibited by applicable law (12 CFR 9.12(e)).

Sales to Related Parties

Property held by a national bank as fiduciary generally should not be sold or transferred, by loan or otherwise, to the bank, its directors, officers, or employees (12 CFR 9.12(b)(1)). Nor should such property be sold or transferred to persons whose connections might impair the bank's best judgment, to organizations whose interests might have that effect, or to affiliates of the bank, their directors, officers, or employees. However, such sales or transfers may be carried out:

- When authorized by applicable law;

- When the bank, as fiduciary, has been advised by its counsel in writing that it has incurred a contingent or potential liability and desires to relieve itself of such liability (the sale or transfer may not result in a loss to the trust account);

- As provided in 12 CFR 9.18(b)(8)(iii) with respect to defaulted securities; or

- When required by the OCC.

The bank's exercise of its best judgment may be affected when:

- The bank uses a broker to sell trust assets to a related party or organization, and

- The sale occurs shortly after the property's acquisition by the broker from the bank.

However, if the bank uses a broker to sell trust assets, and the broker is unable to sell the assets for a reasonable period of time, such as a year, a subsequent sale to a related party or organization will not be presumed to violate 12 CFR 9.12.

The public sale of property held by a national bank as fiduciary does not eliminate the conflict of interest. If a director, officer, or employee is the successful bidder, the sale must be made subject to court approval. A court order should be obtained after full disclosure of the relationship between the bidder and the bank. The sale may be consummated after the court order is obtained.

Purchase of Assets or Services from Related Parties

Banks may conduct fiduciary business using insurance agents, real estate brokers, securities broker/dealers, farm and property managers, appraisers, tax preparers, and other service providers. However, except in the circumstances noted below, banks may not purchase assets or services from related parties for fiduciary accounts unless authorized by applicable law. The exception to this rule is that the OCC does not object to a bank's use of an affiliated broker/dealer to effect securities transactions for fiduciary accounts so long as the broker/dealer forgoes any profit and the arrangement is not prohibited by applicable law.

Related parties include the bank, its directors, related interests of directors, advisory directors, officers, employees, and individuals or organizations with a connection or interest that might affect the bank's exercise of its best judgment. Prior written authorizations from grantors of revocable trusts or beneficiaries of irrevocable trusts would enable a bank fiduciary to deal with a related party provided that the bank makes full and complete disclosure of the circumstances surrounding the conflict of interest.

Use of External Investment Advisory Programs

Pursuant to 12 CFR 9.4(c), a national bank is authorized to purchase services related to the exercise of its fiduciary powers from another bank or entity. The OCC has permitted national banks to engage a registered investment adviser to provide investment advice as a subadviser, providing investment management services to fiduciary customers of the bank.

National banks may also act as a finder, bringing together an investment adviser and its customers for a fee. The investment advisor and customer negotiate a contract between themselves, with no bank involvement. National banks lacking fiduciary powers may engage in this service because they do not act as an investment adviser or exercise investment discretion for any party.

Purchases from Affiliated Underwriting Syndicates

Pursuant to 12 CFR 9.12, national banks may not purchase assets, including securities, from themselves or their affiliates for fiduciary accounts unless specifically permitted by applicable law. In addition, 12 USC 371c-1(b)(1) restricts purchases for fiduciary accounts of securities underwritten by a syndicate in which a bank affiliate is a member while that syndicate exists. Such a purchase, however, is not prohibited under 371c-1 if it was approved by a majority of outside bank directors before the securities were initially offered for sale to the public.

Before purchasing a security for a fiduciary account from an underwriting syndicate in which a bank affiliate is a member, or as part of the board's standards for acquisitions, the bank should evaluate such features of the security issue as price; yield; credit quality; structure, including options and call features; maturity; and sensitivity to interest rate movements. The bank should find out whether any similar issues are available and should compare features.

Real Estate Syndications

Although a bank fiduciary may sponsor limited partnership syndications for its fiduciary accounts or common trust funds, neither the bank nor its employees may participate in the syndication. In the absence of specific approval or consent, the general partner should not be a related interest. Bank fees taken for this activity must be fully disclosed and authorized. Participation guidelines should be established to ensure that only appropriate fiduciary accounts are invested in the syndication.

Conflicts of Interest   Appendix C

Trust Brokerage Allocation and Securities Trading

12 CFR 9.5(a) requires national banks exercising fiduciary powers to adopt and follow written policies and procedures that address brokerage placement practices. In addition, 12 CFR 12.7(a) requires that the bank's securities trading policies and procedures:

- Assign responsibility for supervision of all officers and employees who:
    - Transmit orders to or place orders with registered broker/dealers;
    - Execute transactions in securities for customers; or
    - Process orders for notification or settlement purposes, or perform other back-office securities functions for customers.

- Provide for the fair and equitable allocation of securities and prices to accounts when the bank receives orders for the same security at approximately the same time and places the orders for execution either individually or in combination.

- Require certain bank officers and employees to report to the bank, within ten business days after the end of the calendar quarter, all personal transactions in securities made either by them or on their behalf in which they have a beneficial interest. The officers and employees subject to this requirement are those who:
    - Make investment recommendations or decisions for the accounts of customers;
    - Participate in making recommendations or decisions; or
    - In connection with their duties, learn which securities are to be purchased, sold, or recommended for purchase or sale by the bank.

"Front-running" is using nonpublic information inappropriately to gain unfair advantage in a securities trade. An instance of front-running

---

occurs when a bank employee receives an order to buy or sell a security for one or more fiduciary accounts. Normally, the pending trade involves a large block of securities that, when traded, is likely to affect the price of the security. The bank employee then improperly buys or sells that same security for another account, i.e., another fiduciary account or a personal account, before placing and executing the original order. The bank employee's motive is to gain an improper benefit from an anticipated price movement. This practice may violate federal securities laws and may result in the imposition of civil, criminal, or administrative penalties.

Trading should be fair and equitable to all accounts. Trades should not be placed to favor unfairly any customer or to boost the returns of collective investment funds. Banks should always allocate block trades to specific accounts before executing the trade. Fair allocations of blocks are predicated on accounts' needs; unfair allocations are often predicated on favoring a particular account. Banks must have effective monitoring systems to ensure that trades are fair.

Allocating fiduciary business to a broker based on the broker's deposits or other relationships with the bank is an impermissible conflict of interest. A bank should not direct trades based on the money it earns from that relationship. Such an arrangement constitutes self-dealing and may violate the duty to seek best execution.

Transactions (Buying and Selling) between Accounts

A national bank may sell assets held by it as fiduciary in one account to itself as fiduciary in another account, if the transaction is fair to both accounts and not prohibited by applicable law, such as ERISA. The bank, as trustee, must administer each trust for the exclusive benefit of the beneficiaries and should be prepared to demonstrate the fairness of a transaction between accounts by maintaining documentation demonstrating that:

- Both the selling and purchasing accounts received the best price available at the time of the transaction.

- The transaction was consistent with the objectives of both accounts.

- The transaction was available to all accounts on the same terms and conditions.

- No conflict of interest existed between the accounts and the trustee.

Conflicts of Interest   Appendix D

Soft Dollars and Directed Commission Arrangements

Broker/dealers not only execute orders but also provide other services, such as research. In soft dollar arrangements, a fiduciary or adviser receives these other products and services in exchange for directing its clients' brokerage transactions to the broker/dealer. Since brokerage commissions typically do not segregate these services from the cost of basic order execution, the fiduciary or adviser generally receives these services at no cost. National bank fiduciaries that execute soft dollar arrangements with a broker/dealer may be creating a conflict of interest because they are essentially expending clients' assets to benefit themselves. In determining whether a violation of 12 CFR 9.12 has occurred, the OCC looks to section 28(e) of the Securities Exchange Act of 1934 and subsequent SEC issuances and interpretations for guidance.

Section 28(e) creates a safe harbor for investment advisers, including fiduciaries, that use the commission dollars of their advised accounts to obtain investment research and brokerage services. Because a conflict of interest exists when a national bank fiduciary receives research, products, or other services as a result of allocating brokerage on behalf of clients, the bank must either comply with the safe harbor provisions of 28(e) or provide full disclosure of the bank's policies and practices to its fiduciary clients (OCC Trust Banking Circular 17) and obtain consent.

The safe harbor is available even if the commission paid was not the lowest available if the money manager determines in good faith that the amount of the commission is reasonable in relation to the value of the brokerage and research services provided. The safe harbor does not extend to products and services that are not related to research. In order to fall within the safe harbor, any products and services must provide lawful and appropriate assistance to the investment manager in carrying out his or her investment decision making responsibilities.

In general, for a soft dollar arrangement to fall within the safe harbor:

- The arrangement must be limited to brokerage or research services. If the product or service can be used for research and some other purpose, only its research use is within the safe harbor.

- The services must be provided by a broker/dealer.

- The person selecting the broker/dealer must be the person exercising investment discretion. Directed transactions are not within the safe harbor.

- There must be a good faith determination that the commissions paid are reasonable in relation to the value of the service or product provided.

- Commissions must be used to purchase the service or product.

The most significant guidance on the use of soft dollars was issued in 1986 by the SEC, when it issued a release that clarified that products and services that provide assistance other than research, such as administrative benefits, do not qualify for the safe harbor. See also OCC Trust Banking Circular 25, "Use of Commission Payments by Fiduciaries," which clarifies that the receipt of third-party investment advice could fall under the safe harbor. In that same release, the SEC stated that a computer dedicated exclusively to software that is used for research for the client's benefit was covered in the safe harbor. Banks that receive "mixed use" products or services from a broker/dealer must use hard dollars to pay for that portion of the product or service received that is not related to research.

The SEC's September 22, 1998 "Inspection Report on the Soft Dollar Practices of Broker-Dealers, Investment Advisers and Mutual Funds," identifies current issues and makes recommendations to the SEC to clarify its position and provide additional guidance with respect to soft dollars.

Generally, if a soft dollar arrangement is within the safe harbor, the bank is not required to disclose the arrangement to clients or account beneficiaries. Soft dollar arrangements outside the safe harbor may inappropriately benefit the bank, creating a self-dealing transaction, and would require full disclosure and approval by account beneficiaries or clients. Regardless of whether the arrangement is within the safe harbor afforded by 28(e), it may be prudent for the bank to disclose fully all soft dollar arrangements.

Management should periodically assess and affirm the legality and reasonableness of any soft dollar arrangements. The industry's increased reliance on electronic media to execute trades and deliver research information has raised questions as to whether items such as high-speed phone lines, Internet access, personal computers, or fiber optic cables qualify for the safe harbor. Bank counsel at some banks update management periodically on which investment services he or she believes qualify. Because the safe harbor does not protect a money manager who engages in other improper activities, such as churning an account, failing to seek the best execution, or failing to make required disclosures, the OCC would view such practices to be potential violations of 12 CFR 9.12.

Accounts Subject to ERISA

A fiduciary must also consider restrictions on its relationship with employee benefit plans that are subject to the rules of ERISA. According to section 404 of ERISA, a fiduciary's overriding responsibility is to discharge its duties with respect to a plan solely in the interest of the plan participants and beneficiaries and for the exclusive purpose of defraying reasonable expenses of administering the plan. ERISA also has strict rules regarding self-dealing, conflicts of interest, and the use of plan assets to benefit parties-in-interest.

The DOL considers soft dollars and commission rebates to be plan assets which must be managed in the same manner as other plan assets.

(The companion "Retirement Plan Services" booklet of the Comptroller's Handbook, which has yet to be published as of this booklet's publication date, discusses this topic in more detail.)

Conflicts of Interest   Appendix E

Use of Mutual Funds as Fiduciary Investments

The investment of fiduciary assets in mutual funds should be evaluated as any other investment vehicle under applicable law, including the Prudent Investor Rule or Prudent Man Rule, and the terms of the governing instrument of the trust. Two circumstances give rise to a conflict of interest: a bank's investment of fiduciary assets in proprietary mutual funds and the bank's receipt of fees from an investment company in return for investing fiduciary assets in a mutual fund.

Proprietary Mutual Funds

A bank that invests fiduciary assets in proprietary mutual funds must first consider the legality of the investment. Bank counsel should determine that applicable law allows such an investment. Once the legality of the investment is established, the bank must keep in mind its obligation to act solely in the best interests of account beneficiaries.

Before investing, the bank should make a positive determination that the investment meets the needs of the account. The bank should also document through the annual review process that the proprietary mutual fund continues to be an appropriate investment for the account. Factors such as the performance of the mutual fund, fees charged, liquidity, and the needs of account beneficiaries should be considered and documented as part of the annual review process.

The same level of scrutiny should be applied to mutual funds that are not proprietary when the bank receives compensation for providing services to the mutual funds and the bank has invested fiduciary assets in the funds.

Receipt of Fees from Mutual Funds

Some mutual funds pay fees to third parties to defray the cost of shareholder servicing and administrative services. Such services may include placing orders, processing purchases, processing dividend and distribution payments, and responding to customer inquiries.

A national bank may invest trust assets in mutual funds that pay such fees without correspondingly reducing the bank's trust account compensation, if authorized by applicable law. If applicable law does not allow the trustee to retain fees authorized by rule 12b-1 of the Investment Company Act of 1940, the conflict may be corrected by passing the fees to the accounts that have their assets invested in the fund. National banks are encouraged to disclose 12b-1 fees received from mutual funds to fiduciary accounts. The bank should consider whether to obtain an attorney's opinion to support its interpretation of applicable law. The investment must be prudent and appropriate for the account and otherwise consistent with applicable law.

Accounts Subject to ERISA

Mutual funds occasionally pay fees to employee benefit plans' third-party service providers to offset the cost of shareholder servicing and administrative services. Fiduciaries providing such services and accepting these "secondary service" fees must be in compliance with DOL guidelines governing the prohibited transaction standards of ERISA.

In addition, mutual funds may also pay 12b-1 fees to third parties for services performed in connection with the promotion and distribution of fund shares. The DOL has two advisory opinions in this area that provide guidance for employee benefit plans that are subject to the rules of ERISA.

In Pension and Welfare Benefits Administration Opinion Letter 97-16A, the DOL opined that a record keeper that is not a fiduciary under ERISA could receive 12b-1 fees from an outside mutual fund when plan participants direct the investments. The DOL said further that such an arrangement would not violate section 406(b)(3) of ERISA.

According to DOL Pension and Welfare Benefits Administration Opinion Letter 97-15A, if a bank as directed trustee were directed, in accordance with section 403(a)(1) or 404 of ERISA, to invest in a mutual fund that pays the bank a fee for investing with it, the investment would not be considered a conflict of interest. That is, the trustee would not be dealing with the assets of the plan for its own interest or for its own account in violation of 406(b)(1). The advisory opinion goes on to state that in such a case the "mere receipt by the trustee of a fee or other compensation from the mutual fund in connection with such investment would not in and of itself violate section 406(b)(3)."

In essence, Opinion Letter 97-15A provides that the DOL would not object to plan structures where any 12b-1 or subtransfer agent fees attributable to the plan's investment in mutual funds are used to benefit the plan, either as a dollar-for-dollar offset against the fees paid to the bank in its capacity as trustee or as amounts credited directly to the plan. In such a case, the DOL has opined there would be no violation of ERISA sections 406(b)(1) or (b)(3).

To date, the DOL has not issued a written interpretation expressly focused upon the receipt of 12b-1 fees by proprietary mutual funds. However, litigation initiated by the DOL in 1998 to restrict such activity is consistent with previous DOL guidance in this area. DOL has also stated in Opinion Letter 97-15A that a trustee that advises a plan in which the assets are invested in mutual funds that pay additional fees to the advising trustee would generally violate the prohibitions of ERISA section 406(b)(1).

A national bank receiving 12b-1 or subtransfer agent fees should not rely solely on the DOL Advisory Opinions for guidance, as they are limited to the specific facts conveyed in the letters. Instead, the bank should consult with counsel to determine whether the bank's receipt of fees violates the requirements of ERISA.

(The companion "Retirement Plan Services" booklet of the Comptroller's Handbook, which has yet to be published as of this booklet's publication date, discusses this topic in more detail.)

Conflicts of Interest   Appendix F

Unique Situations Posing Potential Conflicts

Closely Held Companies

A bank that administers as fiduciary a closely held company always must deal with the closely held company at arm's length in order to avoid any conflict of interest or self-dealing transactions. The bank must consider the ramifications of any common directorates with such a company. Bank directors and officers should not acquire an interest in closely held companies that the bank administers as fiduciary.

Employees Serving as Directors. In certain circumstances a bank director or officer may serve on the board of directors of a closely held company that the bank is administering as fiduciary in order to protect the interests of account beneficiaries. However, bank management should consult legal counsel before making such an arrangement. Fees received by bank directors or officers while acting as directors of closely held companies should be remitted to the account. These fees may be retained by the bank (in its capacity as fiduciary) only if authorized specifically by the trust agreement, court order, or written consent of the beneficiaries.

Commercial Lending. Loans from the bank's commercial department to a closely held company that is controlled by the bank as a fiduciary must be made at arm's length.

Valuations. A trustee's fee schedule should address the treatment of closely held companies' securities and partnership assets. The schedule should provide reasonable compensation for the services performed. In the absence of specific language in the fee schedule or when a trustee's fee is based on the market value of a closely held company or partnership, the trustee must ensure that its valuation is reasonable and poses no conflict with the account involved. Fees that are excessive because the bank overvalues an asset reflect a breach of the bank's fiduciary duty.

Trust Assets as Loan Collateral (Private and Commercial Banking)

National banks engaged in private banking may lend to grantors of trusts and secure the loans with assets from trust accounts. Such lending is commonly a commercial banking function isolated from the trust department. When such loans are made, a fundamental conflict of interest exists because a bank trustee with investment discretion must optimize the investment performance of the fiduciary investment portfolio and the bank as commercial lender must conserve the loan collateral. This conflict should be disclosed fully to the trust grantor, and procedures should exist to ensure that the investment officer can fulfill the bank's responsibilities as trustee.

The bank must use caution when financing an outside purchaser of property held in trust. Such bank financing is questionable when the trust itself could take back a note or deed of trust as part of the sale of the property. The bank could be construed as usurping a profitable opportunity of the trust. Because of the complexity of these transactions, the bank should consult with legal counsel.

Units of collective investment funds may not be pledged for bank loans (12 CFR 9.18(b)(8)(ii)). In addition, to the extent pledged trust accounts contain bank stock, or shares in bank-advised investment companies, such loans may be subject to the limits of 12 USC 371c(c). A bank may lend to companies for which it acts as ERISA trustee. However, commercial loans to companies secured by their employee benefit trust assets violate ERISA and may subject the bank to penalties under section 406 of ERISA (29 USC 1106).

Multiple Corporate Relationships

Bond Proceeds. A bank may act in multiple roles when proceeds of a corporate bond issue are used to retire a loan at the bank. A bank, as trustee, must refrain from investing discretionary fiduciary assets in the bond issue. If the bank is also the corporate trustee for the bond issue, the bank places itself in conflict with the interests of the bond holders, itself, and its fiduciary accounts.

Acting as Indenture Trustee and Creditor. A national bank may experience a conflict of interest if a debt security for which it acts as indenture trustee defaults, and the securities are held by discretionary trust accounts. Interpretive ruling 12 CFR 9.100 allows a national bank to act as both indenture trustee and creditor until 90 days after the security defaults, provided the bank maintains adequate controls to manage the potential conflicts of interest.

Self-Promotion. The management of foundations and charitable trusts may allow a trustee to promote civic events and activities. The trustee must avoid using trust or foundation funds to promote its own name, and it should not restrict the list of mailings to its own customer base.

Conflicts of Interest

Appendix G

Reasonable Compensation

Rebates from Overnight Investment

Generally, national bank fiduciaries are not entitled to the interest and dividends earned from an overnight depository investment of trust account assets. In the past, most trust departments received the equivalent of these earnings as reductions in their depository expense billings. This arrangement, which may persist at some banks, evolved from the practice of receiving trust asset interest and dividends in same-day funds and paying out to bank participants for their trust customers in clearinghouse funds. A bank should do one of three things with these rebates:

- Distribute them to the customers whose assets generated the rebates.

- Advance to customers monies equivalent to the rebates, so that they receive interest and dividends on the payable date.

- Fully disclose the rebates and obtain customers' approval for the bank's receipt of them.

Fiduciary Cash Flow

Both principal and income fiduciary cash should be made productive. In the absence of proper approval or consent, bank decisions to leave cash uninvested must be properly supported and documented. Banks should reimburse fiduciary accounts when funds awaiting investment or distribution have been placed improperly in low-yielding or nonyielding deposits.

Under 12 CFR 9.10(b), a trustee may deposit fiduciary funds awaiting investment or distribution in the commercial, savings, or other department of the bank, unless prohibited by applicable law. Employee benefit plan investments should be made in accordance with the conditions in DOL regulation 29 CFR 2550.408b-4. To the extent that the funds are not insured by the FDIC, the bank must set aside collateral that equals or exceeds the amount of the uninsured fiduciary funds. In addition, 12 CFR 9.10(a) requires a national bank trustee to obtain a rate of return consistent with applicable law for those funds held on deposit.

The use of an automated cash sweep is an industry standard. The fiduciary should:

- Be able to document fully the reasons for not sweeping all cash balances.

- Allocate earnings based on actual investment returns rather than on an average balance.

- Obtain either an opinion of counsel that a reasonable fee for cash sweeps is permitted or proper consents and authorizations.

A properly structured cash sweep would not violate 12 USC 92a(d), which generally prohibits persons other than the bank fiduciary from writing checks on trust funds.

According to the DOL's Advisory Opinion 93-24A, bank trustees are prohibited from earning interest on the float when they make check payments to ERISA participants. This conflict of interest can be avoided by fully disclosing the practice during fee negotiations and by obtaining authorization in the trust agreement, or by crediting the float earned to the appropriate ERISA account.

Although cash may be swept temporarily into bank time deposits to await investment or distribution, it is generally inappropriate to invest trust funds in time deposits without proper approval or consent. One year has generally been the benchmark for whether funds are invested or awaiting investment. Long-term deposits are presumed to be permanent investments, although some trust funds can legitimately await investment even longer for reasons such as payment of estate taxes. A facts and circumstances test should be applied to each deposit. The one-year benchmark is a guide rather than a hard-and-fast test for a presumption of self-dealing.

Fees for Tax Preparation and Other Trust Services

Fees for preparing taxes or performing other fiduciary services should be disclosed in the fee schedule. If there are no provisions in the trust agreement or the fee schedule for the trustee to charge for other services, the trustee should look to applicable law or obtain a court order to receive proper remuneration for the additional services performed. Written authorizations from grantors of revocable trusts or beneficiaries are also acceptable, provided the bank makes full and complete disclosure of the circumstances pertaining to the conflict of interest.

Bank Employees Serving as Co-Fiduciaries

A national bank is prohibited, except with the specific approval of its board of directors, from allowing any of its officers or employees to receive compensation for acting as a co-fiduciary with the bank in the administration of any account (12 CFR 9.15(b)).

Financial Benefits from Unrelated Interests

A national bank trustee is prohibited from accepting any financial benefits directly or indirectly when such benefits require the trustee to place trust assets in a particular investment or with a particular party (see Banking Circular 233, "Acceptance of Financial Benefits by Bank Trust Departments" and 12 CFR 9.12(a)).

A national bank that receives a financial benefit from a third party, in exchange for the investment of fiduciary assets with the third party, has a financial interest that may interfere with the bank's ability to select investments based solely on the best interests of account beneficiaries. However, subcustodial, transfer agency, and advisory fees received by the bank from an investment company in which fiduciary accounts are invested are permissible if the fees are reasonable and represent bank services verifiably delivered to the investment company. With respect to employee benefit plan accounts, DOL Advisory Opinion 88-2A states that a conflict of interest does not exist when someone other than the bank fiduciary holds the investment discretion to initiate a sweep.

Termination Fees

National banks may charge reasonable fees for their work in terminating a fiduciary relationship. The bank's fee schedule generally will detail the terms of the charge. However, courts have ruled that established termination fees were unreasonable for the services performed by certain banks as fiduciary, and these banks were instructed to charge a reasonable fee.

Conflicts of Interest   Appendix H

Fee Concessions on Fiduciary Accounts

Many banks offer fee concessions on trust accounts established by current or retired bank directors, officers, employees, or their immediate families. The OCC will not object to fee concessions provided that they are consistent with management's marketing and profitability objectives. The concessions must be granted under a general policy and uniformly applied as part of a compensation package approved by the board of directors. Fee concessions may be granted to surviving spouses on the same terms as to directors, officers, and employees.

Fee concessions may be considered a form of remuneration to be disclosed by a bank that has a class of securities registered with the OCC under section 12 of the Securities Exchange Act of 1934. The OCC has incorporated applicable SEC requirements by reference (12 CFR part 11). Item 402 of SEC Regulation S-K (17 CFR 229.402) addresses disclosures of executive compensation generally, and banks should determine by appropriate review of counsel whether fee concessions would constitute disclosable compensation. Disclosures similar to those previously described may be required of any national bank filing an offering circular under 12 CFR 16, which deals with the registration of bank securities with the OCC.

Banks should maintain a list of bank directors, officers, and employees who receive concessions from their regular fee schedules for fiduciary services. All concessions should be made in compliance with the bank's fee concession policy.

Conflicts of Interest   References

Laws

12 USC 61, Voting of National Bank Stock
12 USC 84, Lending Limits
12 USC 92a, Trust Powers
12 USC 371c-1, Restrictions on Transactions with Affiliates
15 USC 77aaa, The Trust Indenture Act of 1939
15 USC 78, The Securities Exchange Act of 1934
15 USC 78, The Insider Trading and Securities Fraud Enforcement
    Act of 1988
29 USC 1001, Employee Retirement Income Security Act of 1974
(ERISA)

Regulations

12 CFR 9, Fiduciary Activities of National Banks
12 CFR 11, Securities Exchange Act, Disclosure Rules
12 CFR 12, Record Keeping and Confirmation Requirements for   Securities Transactions
12 CFR 16, Securities Offering Disclosure Rules
12 CFR 30, Safety and Soundness Standards
17 CFR 240, General Rules and Regulations, Securities Exchange Act
    of 1934
17 CFR 270.12b-1, The Investment Company Act Rule 12b-1

OCC Issuances

Banking Circular 233, "Acceptance of Financial Benefits by Bank Trust
    Departments"
OCC Bulletin 98-1, "Interagency Policy Statement on Internal Audit
    and Internal Audit Outsourcing"
OCC Interpretive Letter 558, "National Banks' Use of Mutual Fund
    Products"

OCC Interpretive Letter 704, "Receipt of Fees from Mutual Funds"

OCC Interpretive Letter 722, "Receipt of Fees from Mutual Funds"

OCC Interpretive Letter 766, "Purchase of Bonds from Syndicates Bank Participate In"

OCC Interpretive Letter 769, "12 CFR Part 9"

OCC Trust Banking Circular 17 "'Soft Dollar' Purchases"

OCC Trust Banking Circular 25 "Use of Commission Payments by Fiduciaries"

Comptroller's Handbook Booklets

"Community Bank Fiduciary Activities Supervision"
"Community Bank Supervision"
"Examination Planning and Control"
"Insider Activities"
"Internal Controls"
"Large Bank Supervision"
"Sampling Techniques"

DOL Issuances

Pension and Welfare Benefits Administration (PWBA) Advisory Letter 93-24A

PWBA Opinion Letter 97-15A

PWBA Opinion Letter 97-16A

PWBA Prohibited Transaction Class Exemption 77-4

Treatises

Restatement of the Law 3rd, Trusts, Prudent Investor Rule, including Section 170 (Duty of Loyalty) (1992)

Scott and Fratcher, The Law of Trusts (4th ed., 1987), including Section 170 (Duty of Loyalty)